The Year I Stopped to Notice

The Year I Stopped to Notice

Miranda Keeling

Illustrations by Luci Power

ICON

Published in the UK in 2022 by Icon Books Ltd
Omnibus Business Centre, 39–41 North Road, London N7 9DP
email: info@iconbooks.com • www.iconbooks.com

Sold in the UK, Europe and Asia by Faber & Faber Ltd
Bloomsbury House, 74–77 Great Russell Street,
London WC1B 3DA or their agents

Distributed in the UK, Europe and Asia by Grantham Book Services
Trent Road, Grantham NG31 7XQ

Distributed in the USA by Publishers Group West
1700 Fourth Street, Berkeley, CA 94710

Distributed in Australia and New Zealand by Allen & Unwin Pty Ltd
PO Box 8500, 83 Alexander Street, Crows Nest, NSW 2065

Distributed in South Africa by Jonathan Ball
Office B4, The District, 41 Sir Lowry Road, Woodstock 7925

Distributed in India by Penguin Books India
7th Floor, Infinity Tower – C, DLF Cyber City, Gurgaon 122002, Haryana

Distributed in Canada by Publishers Group Canada
76 Stafford Street, Unit 300, Toronto, Ontario M6J 2S1

ISBN: 978-178578-815-4

Typeset in Dapifer by Marie Doherty

Printed and bound in Great Britain
by Clays Ltd, Elcograf S.p.A.

About the Author

Miranda Keeling is a writer and actor. She writes plays, screenplays, short stories, articles and poems, and her writing has appeared in the *Metro*, *Reader's Digest* and 'Tweet-off on the Tyne' for *The Verb*, Radio 3. As an actor she works in radio, voiceover, TV, film and stage. She has appeared on *EastEnders*, *Doctors*, *Emmerdale* and at Theatre Royal Haymarket, and is a winner of the BBC Norman Beaton Fellowship for radio drama.

A Year

Introduction • xi

January • 1

February • 15

March • 31

April • 45

May • 59

June • 75

July • 89

August • 103

September • 119

October • 133

November • 147

December • 163

Acknowledgements • 177

For Duncan and Bea,
with all my love

Introduction

You might be reading this because the cover looked cheerful, or you're frantically searching for a present for a friend. You might just be marking time in a shop because it's raining outside and you don't want to leave yet. Whichever way you found yourself here, hello.

It's the small moments, like the one you're having right now, that make up this book: a woman in a shop opens a book and reads the introduction. Perhaps she is wearing a yellow dress. Her brown hair is curly. It is swept up with a silver clip in the shape of a shark. It is chilly in the shop, and she places the book down to take a knitted green cardigan out of her bag and put it on. The wool is thin at her right elbow. Perhaps a man reads this page. He sits at his laptop in a café, looking at this book online. He has dark red hair. His hands on the keyboard are freckled. He is avoiding work. Underneath the café table, a small elderly dog sleeps across the man's foot – the dog makes short whining noises at something in its dream. Perhaps one of these people is you. Perhaps you are completely different.

Days can feel long, and years fast. Our lives are full, yet at the end of the day when someone asks us what we did, we can barely remember. This book is the result of me stopping to notice the details and finding that ordinary life is extraordinary in its own way. If you're someone who can find the big picture a little overwhelming and needs moments of peace in the storm, or who loves the busy, layered fabric of life and just wants some of it captured to enjoy over coffee, read on.

Everywhere I go, I record what I notice: snippets of conversation, images, an atmosphere. I have been captivated by the everyday since I was very small. I grew up in Yorkshire, the Netherlands, America and London. As my mum and I walked around these places, she would often interrupt a sentence to say: 'Did you see that?' I loved the times it turned out that we had spotted the same, small thing. At art college I studied glassmaking. I made miniature sculptures – if you looked closely at them, you could see worlds of colour inside. I carried a notebook everywhere. I drew the things I saw. Then, about seven years ago, I began writing them down instead. Not everything I see is lovely. I live in the world. But that is not what this book is for. You will find the melancholy and the surreal here, but that's as far as it goes.

On 22 July 2014, an artist, Welbeck Kane, sent me a beautiful illustration of one of my observations. It was of a woman reading a book about tigers. I didn't know him, and I hadn't asked him to do this. I posted the words online, and he responded. Since then, I have received hundreds of drawings from people all over the world, aged 11 to 85. People want to share how they see what I describe. There is something wonderful in this process – I see something, I turn it into words, artists read the words and turn them back into pictures. I'm delighted that one of those artists, Luci Power, has provided the images inside this book. Luci has brought my words to life with her own stunning and unique depictions. You probably picked up this book because of the illustration on the front, by the talented Taaryn Brench. What you read inside will make different pictures, again. Everything in this book is something that I saw or heard in the world. People have got in touch to tell me they have recognised themselves or each other. You might find yourself. Or someone you know.

The people, animals, places and inanimate objects in this book are here to make you laugh, wince, smile, agree, think again, see the familiar, raise your eyebrows in surprise, pause and exhale. Read it in any order, at any time. Themes bind the moments together – I know what I see, but you will find your own patterns. May you remember to stop and notice.

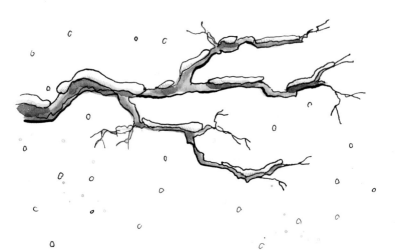

JANUARY

Little girl on the bus: Nice notebook.

Me: Thanks.

Little girl: Is it a diary?

Me: I write about things I see.

Little girl: Like me?

Me: Exactly.

Little girl: Cool.

A man in dirty overalls reaches into the window display of a locksmith's to carefully remove an old glittery plastic Santa for another year.

• · • · •

Man in Finsbury Park: How was the New Year's Eve party?

Woman: I fell in love with a man with a sequinned beard.

A door opens onto a
dark alley and a man in
chef's whites steps out,
does a series of rather
elaborate yoga poses,
and then heads back in.

•·•·•

A cat at the window of a house
watches the rain fall outside
– its large mustard-yellow
eyes bright against grey fur.

Two women in hijab chat and laugh – the tips of their white trainers dancing closer together with the swaying of the train.

• • • •

A little boy on the tube is so worried about his soft-toy lion falling on the floor that he is saying to him, 'Hold on tight, Sycamore Jones!'

Frost best-befriends the grass
in the park, as afternoon light
appears above a line of trees. On
a radio somewhere, 'The Circle
Game' by Joni Mitchell plays.

• • • •

In a churchyard in Hackney, moss
grows on the gravestones, the last
of the sun hits a leafless tree, and
a pigeon settles with a small 'coo'.

A man on the tube resting
his chin on his closed fist
like The Thinker seems
in deep contemplation.
And then, gently, he
begins to snore.

Little boy on the train: Mama?

His mum: Yes?

Little boy: I never see you brush your hair.

His mum: I do a lot of things you don't see.

(Pause)

Little boy: Like flying?

A nightwatchman patrols a
building near Baker Street
in a too-tight suit, the whites
of his eyes gently glowing
from behind iron gates.

• · • •

Against a wall, an abandoned
ironing board leans, cold in
the dark, a deep gash ripped
through its leopard-print heart.

A man walking along Caledonian
Road falls over onto a huge roll of
bubble wrap that he is hugging,
perhaps for just this sort of situation.

• • • •

Bizarrely, at different ends of a
quiet train carriage, two strangers
say rather loudly to themselves
at the same time, 'Still drunk.'

• • • •

A man arguing in a café with his
friend emphasises every point with
a half-eaten banana, its yellow
skin flapping joyfully about.

A woman in a green beret stands in a pub garden surrounded by laughing people as she stares quietly into the glass of white wine in her hand.

• · · •

A woman walks through Tottenham. Her beautiful grey dreadlocks are wrapped into a bun. She stops by an ivy-covered wall and brushes it with her gloved fingers. She looks at the leaves flutter in response. She walks on.

Man on the platform
(looking up from
his book about
mindfulness): Shit.
I've missed my train.

A gentle breeze transforms a
woman's large felt hat – its floppy
beige brim making her suddenly
into a pirate, a cowboy, then a nun.

• · • ·

A builder outside the Shard laughs
as a massive leaf lands squarely on
his bald head, just in time to be
captured in the selfie he's taking.

• · • ·

A woman stands at a bus stop
silhouetted by the Sunday sun, the
vivid green silk of her sari billowing
around her in the wind like smoke.

FEBRUARY

An elderly man in a
blue suit dances slowly
round an empty café.
On noticing me come
in he looks up, smiles
and carries on.

A man sits on the tube. He is very still. His rucksack is printed with comic-book attack sounds like *Boom, Crash, Kapow* and *Blam*.

• • • •

A woman marches through Hackney. She wears red mittens. Embroidered in white wool on the left mitten is the word 'Can' and on the right one 'Can't'.

On a quiet street a mattress rests
like an old boat washed ashore,
its cargo a broken radiator, some
tangled fairy lights and five chips.

• · • · •

A man taking a break from some
sort of conference stands looking
at the rain, a name tag on his
suit jacket reads: un-known.

Woman in a café looking at the heart drawn in her coffee: Shame to put a lid on.

Barista: It's okay. We both know it's there.

Woman: We do.

Little boy on the Heath: Brrriing!

His dad: What was that?

Little boy: The alarm. For chips.

• • • •

A woman cycles along the towpath in the gathering dusk. Behind her runs a small, rather portly, white dog.

Woman (over her shoulder): Keep up, Death Star.

A woman wearing a headscarf the colour of freshwater pearls sits on the steps of a church in Clerkenwell thoughtfully eating Nutella from a jar.

In green and pink chalk letters, on the pavement of a quiet street in Bethnal Green, are written three words: I miss London.

• • • •

A little girl walks through Green Park carrying a hot waffle with chocolate sauce that her dad has just bought her. She blows on it to cool it down and her breath makes clouds of icy white in the cold air.

A boy stands on a
skateboard on Oxford
Street. His hips move
the board left and right.
Snow falls, bright against
the dark paving stones.

A little girl carefully hands imaginary things to her mum, who receives them respectfully – mindful of their fragility.

• • • •

A woman has a floral handbag in the shape of a coffin. She opens and closes it repeatedly, enjoying the feel of its kiss clasp.

• • • •

Over the tiled rooftops of Battersea, a seagull keeps pace briefly with the train I'm on, before dropping away.

Mum walking a pram
full of bags through
Muswell Hill: You
okay, darling? Honey?
(Looks down) Oh! Gosh.
She's in nursery. You're
my shopping.

A woman reads in a café. Her
eyelids are painted with glittery
green eyeshadow. Outside, fog
presses against the window.
In front of her, a collection of
cacti make a desert landscape
of the sand-coloured table.

• · • · •

A white-haired man at a
table by the door smiles
as the waitress perfectly
remembers his favourite order.

Man on the DLR: Are you prepared for today's meeting?

Woman: No.

Man: It's at 9am.

Woman: I know it's at 9am, Dave. And I remain, unprepared.

A woman on the tube in gold heels
and a denim jumpsuit studies a
selection of bejewelled bracelets laid
out in a row upon her left thigh.

• • • •

A man on the tube stands up,
goes to the doors, realises it's not
his stop and sits down again.
Little boy nearby: Embarrassing.

• • • •

A girl cycling in Euston stops
on the pavement to blow warm
air onto her cold hands through
the moth holes in her gloves.

MARCH

Woman on the bus: What
blusher do you use?

Her friend: Oh, cold air,
a brisk walk, alcohol or
sometimes the menopause.
You?

A tiny elderly lady walks through
Willesden. She wears a furry
fuchsia coat and her hair is snuggled
within a purple, polka-dot scarf.
She smokes a king-sized cigarette
without using her hands.

• • • •

A perfect snowflake, worthy of a scientific
photo, lands upon my blue-gloved hand
and gently melts away into the wool.

• • • •

A woman in an old cardigan walks
round an estate in Clapton, tenderly
gathering stinging nettles into a
bag with leather-gloved hands.

A woman gets off the Manchester
Metrolink. Immediately, a different
woman gets on who looks just like her,
and several of us do a double take.

• • • •

Skeins of tan wool lie like pastries
in a shop window in Hackney.

• • • •

Three boy-bumblebees, a teenage-astronaut,
a toddler-fireman and a little girl-rabbi
walk past me on Stamford Hill – all dressed
up in their best costumes for Purim.

Lamps glow at the window of
a pub. A man inside sings karaoke.
A woman outside laughs as she does
an Australian accent by mistake.

• • • •

A man at the back of the night bus
sings 'Imagine' by John Lennon
in a surprisingly lovely voice,
his microphone a mint Aero.

A woman in Soho Square drops
to the ground to avoid a flying
pigeon and her husband thinks,
for a shocked moment, that
she has simply disappeared.

• • • •

A woman on the tube in a yellow dress
leans by an open window between
the carriages, her hair flickering in
the draught created, like flames.

A woman gazing at engagement
rings in the window of a jeweller's
jumps in surprise as her nose
suddenly touches the cold glass.

•·•·•

A lucky-cat figurine sits in a Chinese
takeaway, permanently waving
at us with his tiny golden paw.

•·•·•

With surprisingly lovely poise,
a man working in an empty
health-food shop balances a bottle
of vitamins on the back of his hand.

Hailstones hit the pavement unforgivingly.
A woman shelters two miniature
Dachshunds under her woollen coat.

• • • •

A woman on the bus crochets a fine lace
square with scalloped edges. Intermittent
sunlight falls across her, casting lace
shadow-tattoos upon her arm.

• • • •

A woman in red boots sashays along
Gray's Inn Road, a clipboard in one
hand and on each finger of her other
hand an uneaten Hula Hoop crisp.

A woman cycles through
Victoria Park. She wears a
transparent kagool over her dark
clothes. As it billows out around
her in the wind, she becomes
a translucent-winged creature
flying into this March night.

A mermaid's tail swishes against the
windowpane of a house as I walk past. On
second glance, I see a little girl in a sequinned
jacket, which shimmers in the grey morning
light as she watches the street life go by.

• • • •

Two builders wander slowly through
East London sharing a joke, each
with an oozing fried-egg butty held
in their plaster-splattered hands.

• • • •

A group of ultra-orthodox Jewish men
have set up a table and chairs on the
street to gather together. Large, round,
dark fur hats – their brims lighter in the
sun – decorate their heads like flowers.

A strap from my rucksack gently
taps the back of my leg in the wind,
like the persistent attempts of a
small ghost to get my attention.

• · • · •

A woman and a man walk through
Tottenham. He carries a wooden torso
and she carries two wooden legs and two
wooden arms. All together they make quite
a startling silhouette against the evening sky.

• · • · •

A woman on the train holds
a single cocktail stick, its gold
foil tufts sticking out like the
spitting light from a sparkler.

Little boy watching a cat walk past
him: That cat has some lives left.

His mum (smiling): How do you know?

Little boy: I can see them.

• • • •

Four men in Holborn try so
hard to outdo each other's
head-thrown-back, alpha-style
laughter that one of them falls over.

A man on the train sighs
as, having meticulously
arranged his lunch on his
little fold-down table, the
woman from the window seat
beside him needs the loo.

• · • · •

Graffiti on a café toilet door: I LOVE YOU
(Then underneath): NOT YOU HOLLY

APRIL

Woman on the bus:
I love this time of year.
You can legitimately
eat three hot cross
buns for breakfast.

I sit looking out over Walthamstow Wetlands. A little girl comes to sit beside me. Her mum is catching up.

Little girl: Hello.

Me: Hello.

Little girl (gestures to everything before us): Did you do this?

Me (laughing): No.

She smiles at me as if we both secretly know I did.

A teenager walks through town. On the back of her jacket is a pattern of grey hands, as if she's being guided on her way by several ghosts.

• • • •

Two rosy-faced men sit on plastic bags on the street, improvising harmonies to 'La Bamba' through two orange traffic cones.

• • • •

A man walking through Islington has just burst into laughter, as his attempt to untangle himself from his bag strap and scarf has left him looking like something nobody could solve in the Crystal Maze.

A fishmonger drives his van
through town, windows open.
The drum and bass pouring out
from his stereo intermingles with
a sharply salty smell of the sea.

• • • •

A waiter stands in the
al fresco section of a fish
restaurant, thoughtfully
folding white napkins, under
an intermittently sunny sky.

A telephone engineer with
dreadlocks down to his waist
works at the mass of coloured
wires in a Hackney signal box
with the care of a surgeon.

Stuffed into an air vent on a building in South London, a chocolate wrapper becomes a red foil flower, blooming upon the cold dark metal.

• • • •

A man carries a chandelier through Notting Hill, its crystal droplets catching cold yellow fire in the glow from the streetlights.

• • • •

An old, smashed TV lies on the pavement, its black plastic sides spread out like the wings of a pterodactyl.

A man in the library spreads maps of London out on a desk, the thin paper making delicious crinkling noises under his hands.

• · • · •

A family of four chat in sign language on the train platform and, as their conversation grows in passion, the unique styles of movement from each parent and the two little boys become ever more beautiful as they strike and swoop and float through the evening air.

A man does a handstand in the park while his friend practises walking on a slackline she has hung between two trees.

• • • •

On a moving train, a mum balances like a surfer as she expertly puts her daughter's braids up into neat bunches.

• • • •

A woman in Finchley wears a green coat which is plain on the front and buttoned all the way up the back.

I've no idea how she got into it.

Bus announcer: This bus is on diversion.

Elderly woman to her husband: See? Don't say I never take you anywhere different.

An April breeze lifts the glittery
strands of an abandoned pom-pom
lying on an empty street.

• · • · •

A black dog and a white dog
play reversible chase-me
around the park.

A silver-cowboy-booted pregnant
woman rests a cup of tea on her bump
as she contemplates the pigeons
from a park bench in Soho Square.

• · • · •

A man hired to collect litter
sits smoking by an East London
canal, his high-vis jacket reflected
in the water, his bag of rubbish
forgotten, as he gazes at the swans.

Man on the train: It's that white house. The one I see when we're nearing Cambridge. I feel as if I've lived there. But, of course, I haven't.

• · • · •

A breeze blows fallen blossom across the grey pavement.

MAY

Washing hangs out to dry on a line in my garden. Late May light makes the leaves of a plant by the door translucent and orange-edged. The cat lies on the arm of the sofa beside me, her tabby head lowering into sleep.

Cat at the vet's: Meow.

Man: Yeah, mate.

Cat: Meow.

Man: Yeah, mate, I know.

Cat: Meow.

Man: I hear you, mate, but it's for your own good.

A little girl on the beach
near Rye builds a very
large mound out of sand –
evocative of Sutton Hoo.
Later, when I walk past,
she has just finished
work on a very large hole
where it once stood.

A man's glasses slip slowly down his nose as he reads on the bus and, just before they fall, he pushes them back to begin the process again.

• • • •

A physics student in a bookshop café is explaining 'positive' and 'negative' to her friends in terms of a kitten running towards you or away.

A woman lies on a bench in the Wellcome
Collection reading room, shoes kicked
off, stockinged feet crossed, a book
on her lap. She is close to sleep.

• • • •

The camera lenses of two tourists
in the British Museum clash, as
they simultaneously lean in to
examine the Rosetta Stone.

• • • •

A woman in a shop attempts to
turn the rack of 'Love'-themed
cards around, and the agonised
squeal of the metal puts her off.

A man has stopped on
Oxford Street and stands in
his socks, as he pours what
appears to be green and pink
confetti out of his shoes.

• · • · •

A girl waits to cross the road
in the dark. She wears a black
skirt with a cut-out pattern, and
every time a car's headlights go
past, the holes glow like stars.

In the window of a diner in Montclair, New Jersey, a sign reads: Biggest cookies in the world. A woman standing outside takes one final drag on her cigarette, throws it away and walks back inside.

A man on a clothes stall in
Manhattan steams away
the creases from a dress, as
nearby more vapour rises from
round vents in the road.

• • • •

From my friend's balcony in the
Lower East Side, the sound of
the city is a steady roar of noise.

A woman working in a
chip shop in Hackney lifts
a piece of fish and waits for
the perfect amount of yellow
batter to run off it for frying.

•·•·•

A hairdresser in Islington
washes the hair of a client as she
stares out of the salon window,
shampoo foaming up her arms
like the encroaching tide.

A woman runs at a fast pace through
the park, her dreadlocks swept
up within tight black cloth. Her
expression speaks of how hard
this run is, and how satisfying.

● · ● · ●

Man on his phone at Milton
Keynes Station: Oh okay,
well it would've been good to
have an approximate ETA. I'm
made of coffee and lost time.

A man stands outside some offices
on Oxford Street staring stonily
at a shut glass door in front of him
labelled 'Opens automatically'.

• · • · •

A man sits on the bus drinking
coffee. He wears a white silk taqiyah.
Behind him a woman stares ahead.
Her left eye is milky with cataracts.

Woman in a café looking at her salad: I'm going to ignore the cauliflower.

Her husband: I'm sure it'll be devastated, Maureen.

Set in the concrete of a pavement in Tottenham is the strangely satisfying sight of a single seagull footprint.

• • • •

A woman sitting outside a café stirs her tea, the just-added milk briefly a mini galaxy in the translucent brown water.

JUNE

On a quiet city street, two orangey
pink prosthetic half-legs lean –
their shoes tightly laced, their socks
going see-through in the rain.

Man in a cobbled courtyard
(to three pigeons): What? You
don't want to talk to me today?

·•·•·•

As the ticket gate opens, a tube
worker gives a little nod, as if to say
that both he and the ticket machine
have decided to approve of me.

·•·•·•

Outside a fruit and veg shop in
Wood Green, a little boy touches the
outside of a pineapple suspiciously.

Woman trying on a pair of dungarees
in a clothes shop: I haven't had
dungarees on since I was 18. Oh, that's
because I look like Mario and Luigi.

• · • · •

A woman sits back on her heels at the
edge of the towpath and admires the
brass surrounds of the round windows
on her houseboat, which she has
just polished to a perfect shine.

A man delivers bags of fresh mozzarella to a café. The fat white cheeses float in their water like strange fish.

• · • · •

A very small man screeches to a halt in an old red Mini and parks appallingly, to the soundtrack of psychedelic funk blaring out of his speakers.

• · • · •

There is something intriguing about the sound of a man on the train, who is tapping the table as if playing a piano scale. Then I realise his right hand only has three fingers.

Bus announcer: James Lane.

Woman on the bus (to no one in particular): 'James Lane'. That's nice.

Announcer: Sir Alfred Hitchcock Hotel.

Woman: Well. That's splendid.

With a loud squawk, a large seagull swoops down towards an outdoor café table, picks up a man's bagel in its beak, spills the entire contents of a woman's coffee into her handbag, and flies off again. A waitress from the café yells after it, 'You again! I'll tell management!'

• · • · •

A woman in Brighton insists her husband brings his phone on its selfie stick into the sea. He is not the most relaxed person in the water.

• · • · •

A little girl walks up Brighton beach, carefully carrying an upended plastic water bottle top.

Me: What's in there?

Her (smiling): The sea.

A woman cycles through
Tottenham, her tattooed
legs a fast-moving gallery.

• • • •

A man about to ring the doorbell of
a terraced house stops himself, and
leaves – just before a woman opens
the door and gazes at the empty street.

Woman knee-deep in mud
at Glastonbury Festival:
The trick is to keep moving
or sink without trace.

• · • · •

A little girl in the grounds of
Blenheim Palace keeps trying to teach
herself to curtsy and falling over.

At Finsbury Park Station a
busker suddenly starts playing the
bagpipes and a little boy jumps
nearly half a foot into the air.

•·•·•

A man outside a café drinking a hot
cup of takeaway tea peers mole-like
at London through the fog of
suddenly misted-up spectacles.

•·•·•

Women stand outside a hairdresser's
in Shepherd's Bush smoking cigarettes.
Their hair, entrapped in silver foil,
makes them look part droid.

A woman on the tube,
her beautiful silver hair
cascading in waves over
her vivid red cape, nods
to herself as she reads
a book about tigers.

At Leeds Station a white-haired
man plays gloriously
enthusiastic boogie-woogie
on the public piano.

• · • · •

An American woman in Newcastle is
describing how, when her boyfriend
first asked her to go out with 'us', it
took her a while to understand.

Early Thursday sun begins the
process of heating up my street
as I walk along it. The houses
sit – squat and silent – windows
reflecting my progress back at me.

● · ● · ●

A waitress in a busy café unpeels
the label on a bottle of water
she was drinking from and
sticks it back down askew – a
clear message to her future
self that this bottle is hers.

JULY

In the open kitchen of a deli a
man makes calzoni, deftly folding
the edges down around their fat
bellies with flour-coated hands.

•·•·•

Through the summer
heatwave, the kosher
ice cream van drives
its frozen wares, local
children lifting their faces
towards the sound.

Woman on the tube: How old is your baby?

Mum: She's two and a half weeks.

Woman: Wow. What's her name?

Mum: Still deciding.

Little girl nearby: My name's Martha. (Pause) So you can have that for free.

At King's Cross Station a woman on the platform rocks her bright red suitcase back and forth on its wheels as if soothing a baby.

• · • ·

A woman walks into the station. She wears a top with a pattern of flowers. On her neck is a flower tattoo, as if one of them has escaped.

• · • ·

A little boy being pushed in a pram waves at every person he passes and shouts, 'You're doing so well!'

Man in Margate: Remember that roof my brother fell off last year? He fell off it again the other day. Such a joker.

• • • •

Woman on the bus: Oh, I've just remembered why I'm so tired this morning. It's Eid, innit?

A woman waits in the heat of
a Chinese takeaway. On her
feet are long pale blue socks.
She plays with the laces of
her tall white roller-skates,
which lie across her knees.

• · ◉ · •

A woman walks to London
Pride, her smile wide
and her outfit a riot of
sequins gleaming under
the Saturday sun.

A little boy pets a dog on the tube. He tries to give her some Lego from his pocket.

His mum: No, darling.

Boy: But it's the best present.

• · • · •

A woman on the tube wears ruby-red glittery shoes. Presumably this makes it much easier to get home.

A woman pretends she isn't reading
the book of a man beside her on the
bus, who pretends he isn't holding
it so it's easier for her to do so.

• · • · •

Two parents in a café spend so long
discussing whether to sit outside,
their little boy removes his clogs
and lies down on the floor.

• · • · •

Tall trees cast cool grey
shadows across the hot park.

Man on the tube: I'm tired.

His wife: Oh we're all tired, Brian.

• • • •

Man on his phone: Yes, Faruk? Sure. I have a hundred things on my to-do list. What can I add for you?

A woman works on a laptop in her
narrowboat on the river. The small
French doors are open wide, and
her desk faces the afternoon sun.

• • • •

A tall girl with a silver nose ring
and grey bowler hat strolls through
Stoke Newington, followed closely
by a slinky black, green-eyed cat.

A small brown dog outside
a shop perfectly copies the
subtly shifting head positions
of his owner, as she chats
away inside the shop.

• · • · •

A woman in a silk shirt printed with a pattern
of knives and forks arranges a long blonde wig
on a man in a brightly lit chip shop, badly.

• · • · •

Man on the tube platform: I took
her to Watford. I bought her
popcorn. She hasn't called.

Two men sit down in
a bar, roll up their sleeves
and break open the
travel Connect Four.

• • • •

An old sofa rests in a front garden
– its insides spilling out, like
secrets after too much wine.

• • • •

Man on his phone in Hackney: It's
wunna dem tings, bruv. People just
got to live with sadness sometimes.
It's okay to watch TV until the world
clear. You be out the other side soon.

A wrinkly-skinned dog stands
in the damp of morning
outside a shop. A man comes
out and ruffles the dog's
folds of fur, she gives him a
grumble of joy, and they head
off side by side into Sunday.

AUGUST

A woman walks along a sunny street. As she passes beneath the trees, their shadows stroke her shoulders with their grey fingers.

● · ● · ●

A little girl in Honor Oak Park looks at her just-bitten-into flapjack as if surprised that such an odd-looking thing could taste so nice.

Man in a gallery (observing a security guard): The trouble with modern art is, I don't even know if that's a real man, on an actual chair.

In the ever-changing winds
at Bamburgh Castle, the long
brown hair of a woman looking
over the battlements becomes
a perfect weathervane.

•   •   •   •

Little boy near Alnwick (in rain so
strong it's hard to stand up): It's wet.

His dad: Aye, little laddy. That it is.

A little girl wearing a yellow and white stripy dress shouts, 'Pocket, pocket, pocket, pocket, pocket, pocket!' to her bemused Dad, who clearly doesn't understand the utter joy of suddenly discovering your favourite dress has pockets.

· · · ·

A baby sits in a pram on the tube beside a woman who is sleeping. Between them is a pane of glass. The baby places her hand onto the glass – palm and fingers firm against it. She looks at the woman as if sending her a nice dream, then takes her palm off the glass and looks away.

Man in a café in Durham: What can I get you?

His friend: A coffee.

Man: A fancy one?

His friend: Just a cappuccino.

Man (nods): A fancy one.

As the door of this café opens, a
breeze swirls in, riffles through every
page of my notebook as if looking for
something, and then leaves again.

• · • · •

In a restaurant in Hove a man in chef's
whites suddenly throws a scouring
pad up into the air and catches it,
as if he's just had a brilliant idea.

• · • · •

A man who has been lying on
Brighton beach sits up, pebble
marks disappearing from his
back like a fading memory.

In the morning sun, two girls play Jenga in the park – sitting on the grass, they form a diamond shape between their outstretched legs, trainer toes touching.

On this hot, crowded tube, the prime
standing spot is beside a woman who fans
herself with a large, wood and paper fan.

●·●·●

With extraordinary care, a man on
the bus slowly tears his paper bus
ticket into a perfect fringed skirt.

●·●·●

The white beard of a man
walking through Islington turns
out to be an icing-sugar imprint
from a pastry he is eating.

A dog runs full pelt into
the sea near Whitstable
as a seagull gently floats
towards the shore.

• · • · •

Woman (looking out to sea): Oop,
Grandad's off round the buoy again.

Little girl on the beach (to me): Where are you going?

Me: Swimming in the sea.

Little girl: But you haven't got your armbands on!

A woman steps out of her
house in Camberwell wearing
a fabulous leopard-print
catsuit and empties her small
recycling bin into the big one.

· · · ·

A man in flip-flops and shorts
shelters under an awning near
Oxford Street and watches
the rain with a small sigh.

A bus driver waits as a cyclist
passes in front of him – the single
headlight on her bicycle glares
cyclops-like through the dark.

• · • · •

With a wonderful smashing clash,
a man in a hi-vis jacket squashes
metal trolleys together, as a
supermarket closes for the night.

• · • · •

Bats flit between the August
trees so fast my brain tries to
convince me they aren't there.

A man outside a yet-to-open piano shop signals frantically to the woman inside to let him in. This is clearly a musical emergency.

• · • · •

With a satisfying 'click' a sales assistant puts the head back on a mannequin at Fenwick's.

SEPTEMBER

On a sweltering, packed rush-hour
train, my arm suddenly feels lovely and
cool, and I look down to see a shopping
bag held by the woman beside me –
full of just-bought cartons of milk.

● · ● · ●

People move slowly through the
city heat. A storm is coming.

An elderly man in a grey tracksuit
jogs continuously on the spot in an
empty chicken shop in Clerkenwell.

• · • · •

A cyclist pulls to a sharp stop along
the canal, the honk-squeal of his
brakes causing the nearby geese to
accept him as one of their own.

• · • · •

A woman walks through Holloway.
A bright wave of grey hair sweeps
through her otherwise jet-black
curls, like a glimpse into the future.

A man in the park fills an empty tobacco
pouch from the ends of thrown-away
cigarettes, laying the brown threads
across a newspaper open on his
lap before gathering them up.

● · ● · ●

A man shakes his takeaway chips to spread the salt.

● · ● · ●

A woman on the bus, playing with
a hairband on her outstretched
palm, creates: a helix, an
uncurling fern, a wave.

Wind whips through the tall trees in
the park with a sound like breaking
waves as a single yellow leaf leaps
to join the others down below.

· · · ·

A man at Embankment Station waits
for the train. Lost in thought, he makes
a church and steeple with his hands.

· · · ·

A woman buying a coffee in Victoria
Station reaches for the sugar with
her right hand and gracefully
counterbalances by lifting her left leg.

A little girl stands on the street in Tottenham. She wears an orange jumper, black tutu, silver shoes and a determined expression. She ignores shouts from her mum to 'Stop being silly and come back in the house – it's only spinach.'

A woman walks through King's Cross
Station. A squiggly blue tattoo on
her elbow makes it look as though
she has leant on a child's drawing.

· · • ·

Tufts of green grass cling with
enviable tenacity to the bare,
post-heatwave earth of Soho Square.

· · • ·

A dad cycles through the park
with his little girl, both of them
saddle-bopping to the 90s
hip-hop playing on his phone.

A woman outside a café in Muswell Hill moves to a different chair to find some shade as, behind her, a woman at another table moves to find the sun.

• • • •

A one-armed woman on the bus with a cloud of grey hair reads a book against her knee, the cover of which is a sky at sunset.

• • • •

As the sun sets, a man waters his rainbow chard on the grounds of a Hackney estate.

A man stands outside the front
door of a terraced house. He
minutely adjusts his hair. He lifts
up a bunch of flowers.
He inhales. He rings the bell.

A teenager embarrasses his friend by
singing pop songs in a falsetto as they
walk through the park in the twilight.

• • • •

A woman glides round Tesco's
in blue flip-flops, gold socks and
a red dress, her basket entirely
full of tinned tomato soup.

• • • •

A woman on the tube wears an
astoundingly pink jumper beside a
woman who's either asleep or unable to
open her eyes so close to that colour.

A man struggling solo to put up a
huge sign outside an office gives
up, sits down and lights a cigarette.
The sign says: Team-building.

• · • · •

A woman on the tube wearing lots
of silver jewellery holds one finger
over her closed lips as if to stop
herself from uttering her thoughts.

• · • · •

A man sweeping the floor of a
closed-for-the-night hairdresser's
lifts the broom to also gently sweep
the cat, who clearly appreciates it.

Outside a pub in Islington, a gust of wind rolls a small metal slinky across a table. A woman catches it in both hands and opens it up like an accordion, a smile of surprise on her face.

• · • · •

A man sits on the bus. He has long dark hair, wears a green velvet coat and silver boots and is drinking what appears to be sherry from an antique sherry glass.

A man steps on a loose paving
stone and it see-saws underfoot,
with the soft, sloshing sound
of collected rainwater.

· · · ·

A man cycles past me in the park. He is
wonderfully rotund. He has curly white
hair and wears green trousers. A few
autumn leaves fall around him. From
a little speaker on his bicycle floats:
'I believe in miracles ... you sexy thing ...'

OCTOBER

Man in a tube station lift: Have you thought about New Year's Eve yet?

Woman: No, Sanjay. Give me a moment to get my head around October.

A woman sits on the bus, the white plastic takeaway bag on her lap with its tied-together handles looking remarkably like a bunny rabbit.

•・•・•

Graffiti sprayed on a wall spells out: I love Katie. In newer paint beside it are three more words: So do I.

•・•・•

A woman gets onto the bus. On her cardigan is a pattern of black cats jumping, as if for the sushi she holds in her hand.

Man on his mobile on the bus:
Stick the kettle on would you,
Keith? I'm nearly home.

• • • •

A waitress in a closing café clears
the tables around the island of
a man on his laptop, his screen a
pool of light in the dim room.

A woman walks through town in a
voluminous coat. Tied to the front
of her trolley like a ship's figurehead
is a small, grey cloth elephant.

• · • · •

A little girl on a doorstep manages
to negotiate eating an entire
piece of toast while having her
coat put on by her mum.

• · • · •

A man on the tube stares at the
pink hair of a woman opposite
him as if trying hard to understand
an especially difficult puzzle.

Along the towpath in Tottenham,
well-worn dips in the earth
wait for the rain to come. They
are the puddle catchers.

• · • · •

A stout white dog with a patch of black
fur around her eye runs alongside me as
I walk along the River Lea. From behind
me, a woman shouts, 'Laura, stop flirting.'

A woman walks up to the glass door of the café I'm in. She wears a bobble hat. With one hand on the glass, she turns and takes a last look out at the rain, before pushing the door and walking slowly in.

A little boy in a pub in Durham absolutely
collapses into peals of laughter every
time he looks at his plate of chips.

● · ● · ●

Seagulls swoop and soar above,
as teenagers in the park turn
various parts of a bus stop into
percussive instruments.

● · ● · ●

A man sighs as he turns the key in
the ignition of his knackered old van,
on the side of which is written:
As good as it gets.

A bespectacled man in the window
of a café in King's Cross holds
his hands as if in prayer over his
fancy Halloween-themed latte
with swirly cream on top.

• · • · •

A cyclist walks through Ridley Road
Market and, before I see him, I hear
the small sounds he makes on the
pavement with his clip-in cycle shoes.

• · • · •

In a late-night salon near Dalston a woman
arranges long glossy extensions on a table
ready to weave into her client's hair.

I wait for my train to be announced
at Victoria Station. Endless streams of
people walk in all directions, their shoes
squeaking against the polished floor.

• • • •

Rain throws itself onto east London.
The vast green leaves of a banana tree
in someone's garden bend under the
onslaught. In the distance, a green
church spire pierces the grey sky.

Two men carrying one bar stool each through town keep stopping to sit on them for a chat before carrying on down the road.

• · • · •

In an empty shop, a lone sales assistant tries on several sparkly necklaces at once and poses in front of the mirror.

Man on a bus: I did my kids'
Halloween make-up. They loved it,
but it scared their friends. I might have
overdone it. I'm a trauma surgeon.

● · ● · ●

Watching the city traffic whizzing by,
four women dressed as cats sit on the
pavement, feet in the road, sharing some
shop-bought fruit between them.

● · ● · ●

A man in a grey suit sits in a quiet
café opposite a woman wearing
vampire teeth, who struggles
to eat her noodles with poise.

Mum (shouting at three children who have reached the road): Stop!

The children pose together as if suddenly frozen in a fierce wind.

· · • · •

The clocks change and, suddenly, like a great bird, night spreads her wings over the late October sky.

NOVEMBER

Fireworks explode around
Tottenham, making the
air crack and sparkle
with staccato sound.

• · ◆ · •

A woman shivers as she collects
finished breakfast things from the
tables outside a café, her breath
swirling like smoke in the cold air.

A woman walks through Chancery Lane. Pinned to the collar of her navy parka is a handmade poppy, a shiny black button at its red knitted heart.

· · ◆ · ·

A little girl in a shopping centre spins round and round, enjoying the feel of her dress widening out with centrifugal force.

· · ◆ · ·

Teenager on a bus (watching the sleet fall outside): I like mangoes. The best ones are in my grandmother's garden in Ghana. They are like sunshine.

As the sun rises, a man stands on a busy road by Warren Street Station, wearing what looks like a pair of pyjamas and biting into a piece of buttered toast.

• · • · •

A toddler in a café is presented with her hot milk (it has marshmallows on it): Oh, Mummy! Thank you. You have bought me some ... stones.

• · • · •

In the sudden rush of air created by an oncoming train, two white paper bags race each other almost all the way to the top of an escalator.

Music leaks out of the headphones of two passengers in this tube carriage, weaving an uncomfortable tapestry of contrasting beats.

· · · ·

A woman holding her phone in the bitter cold touches the tip of her nose to the lock screen, checks to see if anything has happened, sighs and removes a glove.

A woman on the tube
in a mint green jumper
drinks a massive cup of
coffee. Her bird-like face
carries an expression of
waiting for it to kick in.

The wind flings leaves over a road
in Clapton as if they were fleeing
a zombie-leaf apocalypse. One hits
the bus window and slides down.

• · • · •

A figure walks across
the Heath in the gloaming,
dark against the damp grass.

Woman in Stoke Newington: If they can clone dogs, could I clone my cat?

Man: I doubt it.

Woman: Why?

Man: Everything's more difficult with cats.

A man cycles an empty rickshaw through Covent Garden, a large, plastic, light-up pink heart blinking brokenly on the back.

• · • · •

A woman working in Daunt Books in Kensington reaches into the window display of large, silver baubles with a grabber, to retrieve a dropped book.

• · • · •

The lights of a late-night launderette shine onto a woman as she unloads washing from one of the huge metal machines.

Man in South Kensington: As a matter of fact, many people are jealous of my beard.

•·•·•

On a street corner, three solemn-looking men stand together in deep silence. One of them reverently holds a ginger cat tea cosy.

•·•·•

Pursued by a pigeon, a woman in pink suede shoes walks rapidly through Billingsgate, hiccuping steadily the whole way.

A woman in a forest green coat
walks through Lincoln's Inn Fields;
a brilliantly shining brooch of
exploding stars decorates her lapel.

• • • •

Evergreen trees lean outside
a shop, their prickly pine
fingers trapped within
transparent nets.

• • • •

A woman on Old Street attempts to
hail a taxi, wearing so much gold tinsel
wrapped round herself that she has
trouble even holding her arm out.

A woman in a café angrily tells a friend about her colleagues, representing them on the table as she talks with individual pieces of Monster Munch.

• · • ·

An elderly lady who is taking ages to find her bus pass in her tiny handbag looks up at the waiting bus driver, smiles and says, 'Enchanté'.

A woman with a neat grey bob discusses pastries with a café owner, her thumb carefully holding her place in a book.

• · • ·

Two teenage boys in slippers and pyjamas examine an expensive motorbike outside their house, oblivious to the cold air.

A small boy on the bus carefully eats
the head and all the limbs from his
gingerbread man and passes it to his little
sister, who finishes off the middle.

⚫ · ⚫ · ⚫

From an ancient plastic bucket, a man
pours water over the step of a shop
in Bishopsgate, his morning whistle
muted by the bus window glass.

⚫ · ⚫ · ⚫

Mice run across the tracks at Covent
Garden Station, their little brown
backs shivering with desire to keep
ahead of the oncoming trains.

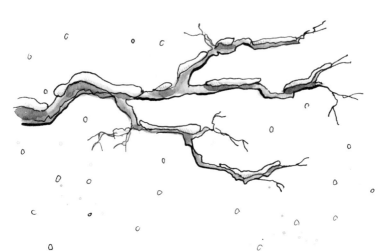

DECEMBER

Two men sit outside a café in the dark, the last of the autumn leaves swirling around them. They are playing chess. One man rests his head in his palm. The other reaches for a piece.

• • • •

Like an opening fan, five people at a bus stop lean sequentially to the left as they try to read the number of the bus coming up the road.

Little girl in Stoke Newington (pointing to the large red birthmark on a woman's face): That's nice.

Woman: Thank you. I'm glad you like it.

• · • · •

A woman and a man meet at Dalston Station, realise they are both carrying a bunch of flowers for each other and, laughing, exchange them.

Woman in a bakery: You were in my dream last night.

Man: Oh?

Woman: In a red Mini. You drove off and left me in the rain.

Man: Oh. Sorry.

(Silence)

As a festive decoration, a man in
Camden has decided to tie an enormous
red lace bow around his front door
and is now struggling to shut it.

• • • •

A woman waits for a bus in Clapton. She
wears a black burka, accessorised with
electric pink Santa-patterned mittens.

• • • •

A little girl is being walked through
the park in a pram. She wears a red
woolly hat and leans forward in her
seat as if watching the final minutes
of a tensely close football match.

Three small children walk arm in arm through Hampstead Heath. With a brilliant smile, the middle one suddenly shouts, 'We're together!'

• • • •

A man on the tube recognises the kind-faced woman with white hair opposite him as his teacher from school and re-introduces himself after 25 years.

• • • •

A woman sits on the bus. Her phone rings. The ringtone is the *Doctor Who* theme tune. A little girl nearby nods her approval.

Woman in Canary Wharf: Oh I take Christmas very seriously. Make my own mince pies. Tinsel. Wear a reindeer outfit to church. The lot.

• · • · •

A man runs for a bus, the wood and leather toggles on his duffle coat swinging towards each other and away – inaccurate trapeze artists.

A man outside a pub checks his reflection
in the window, before reaching into
his pint and proceeding to smooth his
eyebrows down with beer.

• • • •

Two tipsy builders walk through town
singing Willie Nelson's 'Georgia'
– one wearing a Santa hat and the
other a scarf made of bubble wrap.

• • • •

A man walks through Holloway
carrying a Christmas tree
and a baby. He makes a small
attempt to run for a bus, before
laughing at even trying.

A woman on the bus twists a
section of her hair, places it
between her lip and nose like
a moustache, and begins to read.

• · • · •

A man planes wood outside a joiner's
on West Green Road, dust rising like
smoke, as the day outside fades to grey.

A teenager sleeps on the bus, conversing in quiet mumbles with a person in his dream.

• • • •

A woman on the train meticulously brushes crisp crumbs from her smart black trousers onto the lap of the man beside her.

• • • •

An elderly lady shares a laugh with a teenager as they spot a brand new toilet left by the bus stop, as if waiting for a bus.

A builder waiting at the bottom of
some scaffolding amuses himself
by pretending his gloved hands
are puppets having an argument.

• • • •

With a surprising amount of noise,
a little red hair clip is suddenly
run over on a busy road.

A man reads a book in a quiet café
in Peckham, a small rust-coloured
puppy asleep over his shoulder.

• • • •

Two men walking their babies
along Regent Street competitively
check out each other's pram.

• • • •

A woman on the tube carefully
lifts up her perfect fringe, applies
headache relief gel to her forehead,
replaces her fringe and exhales.

Through the misty morning
bus window, the colours
of the city melt into each
other, like spots of ink
dropped close together
onto damp cloth.

Acknowledgements

Firstly I would like to thank my brilliant editor Kiera Jamison for her confidence in me, for all our wonderful conversations about observing life and for her sharp eye for detail. And thank you to the excellent team at Icon Books. Thank you, Dylan Keeling, for being my wonderful brother and a huge inspiration to me both as a writer and a person. Michael Keeling, thank you for your clarity on this text, for teaching me to ride a bike when I was 4 and for everything in between. Lucy Keeling, you have always been and are still my guiding light. Ceiwnen McMillan, thank you for your encouragement and your editor's perspective on it all. Katrin McMillan, thank you for your joyous enthusiasm about this project. Thank you to my wonderful teachers Maggie Hamand, Howard Cunnell and Naomi Wood from whom I learnt so much and without whom I wouldn't have begun calling myself a writer. Thank you, Moose and Karen Allain, for being a positive presence throughout, from my early tweets until now. Thank you to the fabulous Harry Myers and Anna Strickland, you both know how much you have been part of this. To my cat Maple, thank you for being just grouchy enough to make being allowed to hang out with you a privilege.